Habitats

CW01665666

By the end of this book you will know more about:

- Sorting living things in a variety of ways.
- Habitats and organisms that live in them.
- How to explore conditions in habitats.
- How some plants and animals are adapted to their habitat.
- Food chains.
- How habitats change and how to protect them.

You will:

- Use measuring equipment.
- Plan and carry out a fair test.
- Use books and ICT to find information and use and make keys.

Plants and animals are different.

Tree

Task 1 *All sorts of living things*

- How many living things can you think of? Make a list.
- How do you know if something is either a plant or animal?
- What should you look for? Write down your ideas.

Bluebell

Plants and animals come in all sorts of shapes and sizes.

Most plants have green parts but animals are not often green.

All plants and animals grow and have babies or make more plants.

Rabbit

Daisies

Snake

Horse

Task 2

What is a plant? What is an animal?

Emily and her friends looked at the pictures of plants and animals on page 2.

They had to work out which were plants and which were animals.

They talked about what they had seen.

Here are some of their ideas.

- Do you think the children are right or wrong? Explain your ideas.
- Set out your work like this.

Different animals are found in different habitats.

Task 3 *Sorting living organisms*

1,2

An **organism** is anything that is or once was alive.

- Make a list of the organisms in this picture.
- Cut out the cards on Task Sheets 1 and 2. Sort the organisms into plants or animals.
- Tell the class how you sorted them.
- Can you sort your list of plants and animals from the picture into groups?

Plants	Animals
dandelion	squirrel

Words to learn and use:
animal
organism
plant

Task 4

What is a habitat?

A **habitat** is like the address of a living thing.

Look at the address of Brock Badger.
He lives in his sett (den) in an oak wood.

The oak wood is his habitat.

- Find or think of a plant or animal in or near your classroom. Write an address for your plant or animal on a postcard.

Brock in his habitat

Extra Challenge

Habitats can change. These changes can affect the plants and animals that live in a habitat.

- The picture below shows a habitat as it was 10 years ago and as it is now. How has it changed?

10 years ago

Now

- Now draw and write to show how the habitat of your plant or animal could change.
Show how this would affect your plant or animal.

Task 5 Different types of environment

Habitats, and the plants and animals in them, are affected by the conditions around them. These conditions are called an **environment**.

There are many types of environment such as seas, forests and towns. They are different from each other because their conditions - how cold, wet, dry, light, dark they are - are different.

Here are some different environments.

Wetland

Tropical forest

Desert

- What would the conditions in these environments be like?
- What living organisms might you find in these environments?
- Make a list. Use a table like this:

Environment	Conditions	Living organisms
tropical forest	wet, hot	

Task 6

Habitat search

The children in the picture are studying different habitats.

- Think of some habitats in or near your school.
- In groups, visit each habitat. Take a note book and pencil.
- Make a list of the habitats you visit. Share your list with other groups.
- Try to sort your habitats by size.
- Try to sort your habitats by the different living organisms in them.
  Use a table to record your groupings.

Task 7

Habitat estate agency

- Choose one of the habitats you visited.
- Make a brochure or leaflet advertising this habitat to a plant or animal.
- Before you start, think about:
  - a name for your habitat
  - the address of your habitat
  - what pictures to use, for example, drawings, photographs
  - words to describe your habitat, for example, light, dark, dry, wet.
- How could a computer help you with this task?

Predict what organisms might be found in a habitat. Observe a local habitat and record the animals found.

Task 8

Scientific Enquiry

Sampling the habitat

3

You can find out more about living organisms in habitats near your school by asking questions. Emily and Darren looked for animals in some dead leaves.
Here are some questions they asked.

What animals might you find in dead leaves? Why?
Make a list.

Emily and Darren could not search all the dead leaves in the wood. Their teacher showed them how to take **samples** using a P.E. hoop.

Emily and Darren threw the hoop under two different trees: an oak and a beech tree.

They carefully and quietly searched the dead leaves.

They made a table showing the animals they found and describing what the environment was like.

Sample your habitat like Emily and Darren.
Record your findings in a table using Task Sheet 3.

Task 9

Scientific Enquiry

Getting more information

4,5,6

You can find out more about your habitat by measuring:

- how much water is in the ground
- the temperature within the habitat
- the amount of light reaching the habitat.

Practise measuring the water, temperature and light in different habitats by completing Task Sheets 4, 5, 6. Agree with your partner the measurements before recording them.

Now look at your results.
Answer these questions.

1 Which habitat was the coldest or warmest?

2 Why do you think this was?

3 Which habitat was the driest, dampest or wettest?

4 Why do you think this was?

5 Which habitat was the lightest or darkest?

6 Why do you think this was?

Extra Challenge

Use these results to add more information to the brochure you made in Task 7.

Task 10

Brownhill Wood

Brownhill Wood has many different types of tree including oak, ash, holly, beech and sycamore.

Some children investigated the beech and oak areas of the wood. They collected information about the temperature, light and soil water.

Trees in Brownhill Wood

Beech Area

The temperature was 6°C, the amount of light reaching the ground was 5 units (very shaded) and the soil water measured 1·5 units. We found only two spiders under the beech trees.

Oak Area

The temperature was 8°C, the amount of light reaching the ground was 10 units (much less shaded than the beech area) and the soil water measured 3 units. We found many earthworms, spiders, insects and woodlice.

How could they present their results in a better way? Discuss your ideas, then show how you would present them.

Extra Challenge

Compare the oak area of the wood and the beech area.

Write your answers to these questions.

1 How are the temperature, water and light different?

2 Where do most insects and spiders live?

3 Why do you think the children decided to take measurements of the temperature, light and soil water at the same time?

4 What else could they investigate?

Living things are adapted to their environment.

Task 11

Creatures in cool places

- Read the Fact File.
- Make a table to show how you think each animal has **adapted** to living in a cold environment.
- Look at your table.
  How are these animals similar?

Fact File

Animals that live in cold environments

Plants and animals are found all over the world in hot, cold, dry and wet places. The organisms in an environment are often specially suited to live in that environment. For example, a frog has webbed feet suited to life in a pond. The frog is **adapted** to its environment.

These animals live in very cold places. They are adapted to a cold environment.

A polar bear is very big and has thick white fur. Its ears are small and its feet large. Some of its teeth are very sharp and pointed. It eats mainly seals.

The Arctic hare has a fur coat and big feet. Its ears are shorter than hares that live in warmer places. It has sharp front bottom teeth. It eats plants.

The Arctic fox has thick fur, short ears and hairy foot pads. It has sharp front and side teeth. It usually eats small animals, eggs, plants and polar bear leftovers.

The seals that live in very cold seas have short ears and a short nose, thick fur and a very deep layer of fat under the skin. They have a tapering body and eat fish, shrimps and other sea creatures.

Task 12

Scientific Enquiry

How animals adapt

- Invertebrates are animals that have no backbone. Ask your teacher to help you make a collection of invertebrates like these.

Woodlouse

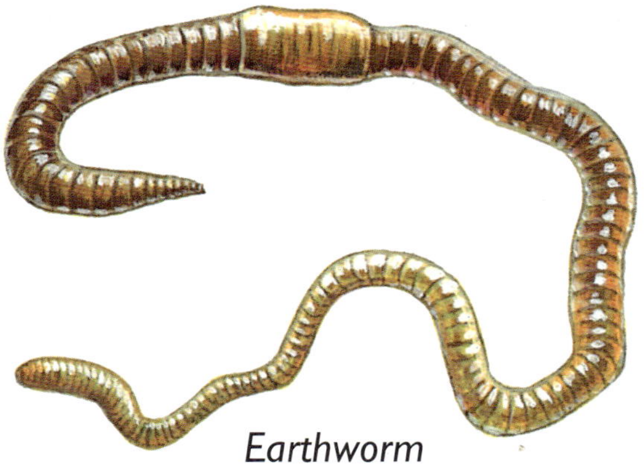

Earthworm

- *Always put animals back where you found them.*

- Look at the animals closely.
  - Where do they prefer to live?
  - What is this place like?
  - Why do they prefer it there?
  - What special feature do they have which helps them to live where they do?
  - How does the way they behave help them to survive?

- Draw and write to show your ideas.

Snail

Slug

- Choose an animal
- Make a large drawing of your animal.
- Add information to show where it lives and how it has adapted to live there. Use books, CD-ROMs, and the Internet to help you.

Group organisms by how they look.

Task 13 *Dear Worm*

- Choose a pair of animals from this list.

centipede and slug
woodlouse and blackbird
tadpole and ladybird

The Greenway
Allotment Place

Dear Worm

How can you live in soil for so long?

It is very dark down there. I would not find many juicy leaves to eat. It would be very rough moving around in the soil and stones, and I do like the smooth surface of big green leaves or paving stones. I expect it is nearly always damp and that might suit me. I try to keep my skin moist all the time. When it is very hot and dry, I have to go into my shell so that I don't dry up. This is when the birds might find me, although the colours of my shell match my habitat so I am well camouflaged.

Yours sincerely

Snail

- Write a letter like this, from one animal to another.

Task 14 *Grouping organisms*

- Look at these pictures or use a collection of invertebrates and some plants from your habitat study.
- How are they similar (alike)? Different?
- How could you group those that are alike? Why would you group them like this?

Task 15

Naming living things

Look at these plants.

The white flower is a wood anemone. Some facts about it have been written for you.

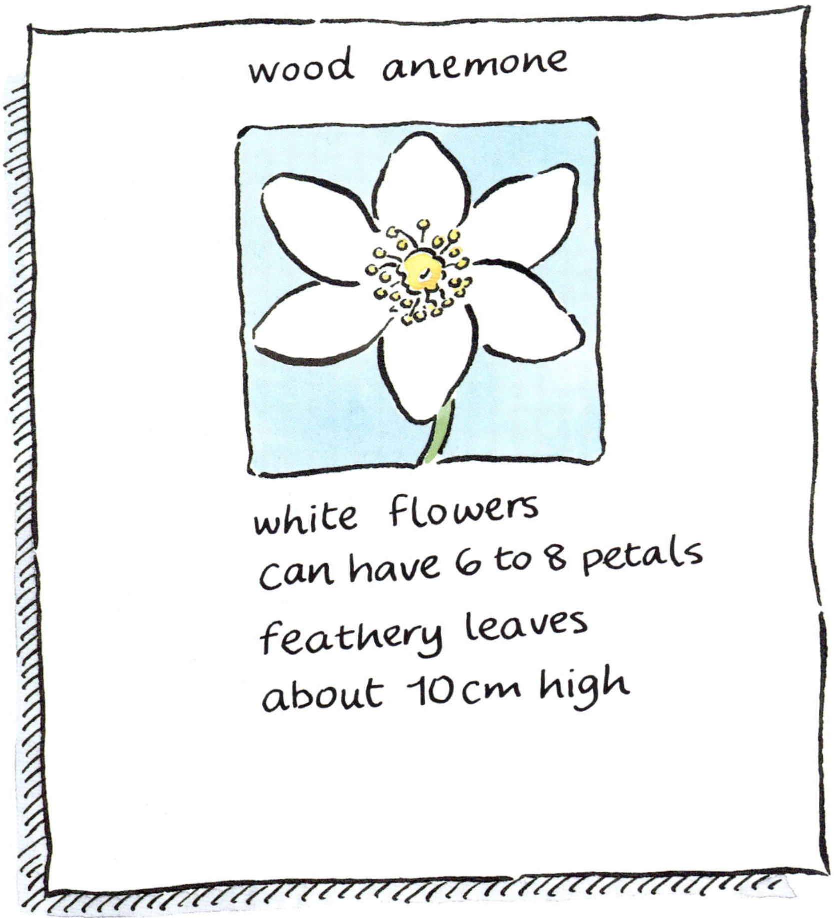

Write some facts about the two other plants. Use books to find out their names.

Use a key to identify plants and animals.

Task 16

What are keys?

7

Some books use **keys** to help you find out the names of living organisms. Keys are easy ways of **identifying** (finding out the name of) an organism when you don't know what it is.

A 'Yes-No' key works by asking questions which have the answer either 'yes' or 'no'. It will lead you to the name or type of organism.

Look at this key. It will help you to name the invertebrates in the pictures.

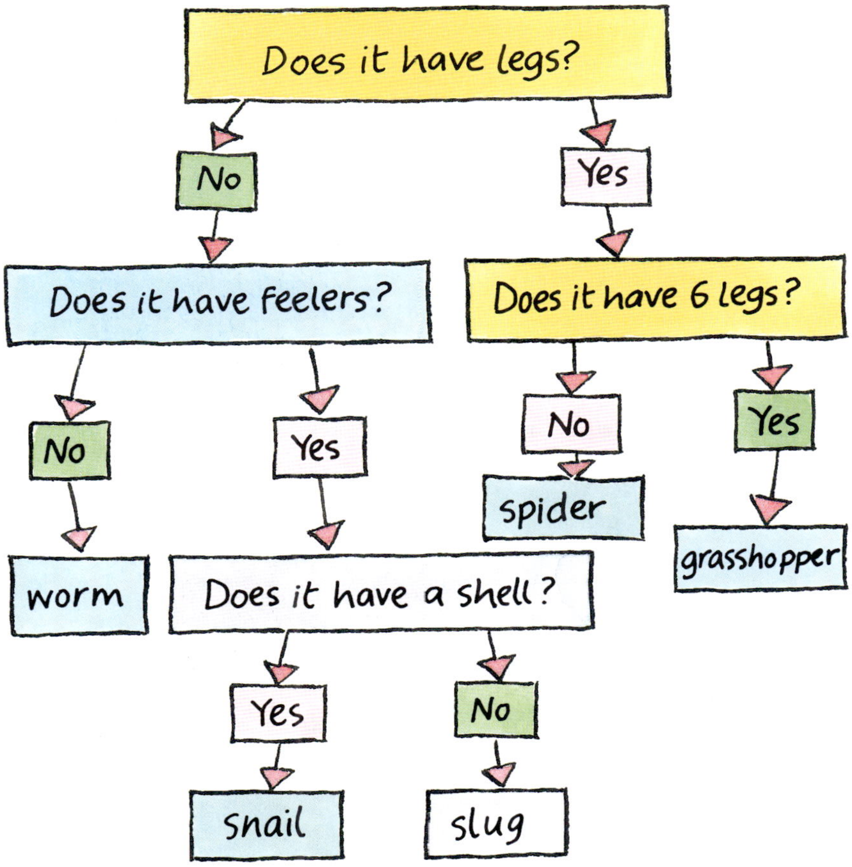

1

2

3

4

5

Now complete Task Sheet 7.

YOU NEED:

snails

lettuce leaves

pieces of apple

plastic tray or tank

Task 17

Scientific Enquiry

Snail investigation

8

Class 4 raised some questions that they might use for an investigation. The questions were about animals they had found in different habitats.

- The children used a planning board.
- Use Task Sheet 8 to plan and carry out your own investigation of Aruna's question.
- When you have finished the enquiry, discuss your results.
- Do your results help you to answer the question?
- Try to explain your results. Do your results fit what you thought might happen?

Identify food sources of different animals.

Task 18 *Food for animals*

- Choose an animal. Find out what it eats. Use books and CD-ROMs to collect the information.
- Think about sharing your research by designing a poster or making a class book.

Task 19 *Where do animals get food from?*

a

- Look at these pictures showing the story of an egg.
- Draw the pictures in the correct order on Task Sheet 9.
- Use some animals you researched for Task 18. Where does their food come from?
You have now worked out some food chains.

Extra Challenge

- Look at this picture and then draw your own meal.
- Trace each food back.

Fact File

Food chains in the wild

In spring, frogspawn (eggs) hatches into tadpoles. The tadpoles are food for other animals in the pond. The frogs lay lots of eggs, so that there is more chance that some will not be eaten and so they will grow into adult frogs.

Young tadpoles eat green pondweed. Pondweed, like most plants, can make its own food using sunlight. It is a **producer**.

Water beetles eat tadpoles and other small animals. Tadpoles and water beetles can't make their own food so they have to eat other things. They are sometimes called **consumers**.

Some water beetles are eaten by bigger animals like fish.

A **predator** is an animal that eats other animals. The animals that a predator catches are called its **prey**.

Identify a food chain.

Task 20

Predators and prey

A food chain shows you how living organisms in a habitat depend on each other for food. For example this food chain starts with grass which is eaten by a wildebeest which is then eaten by a lion.

Plant — *Eaten by animal* — *Eaten by another animal*

- Read the Fact File on page 18.
- Look at this picture of a pond. Try to work out the food chain in the pond.
- Which are the predators?
- Which are the prey?
- What would happen if there were no plants in this pond?
- Starting with a plant, draw some food chains of your own.

Most food chains start with a green plant.

Task 21 *A garden food chain*

A greenfly has a mouth like a syringe.
The greenfly makes a hole in the vein of a leaf or plant stem with its mouth.
It sucks the sugary liquid from the plant.
Greenfly are eaten by insects such as ladybirds.
Ladybirds are eaten by birds.

- Draw this as a food chain.
- Spot the producer, prey and predators.

Extra Challenge

- Choose a habitat you have studied.
- Find out the foods of some animals that live there. Use books and CD-ROMs to find out the food chains in your habitat.
- Draw the food chains. Show these:
  - Producers
  - Prey
  - Predators

Make sure the arrows point from a plant to an animal and from prey to predator.

Words to learn and use:
adapted
consumer
environment
food chain
invertebrate
key
predator
prey
producer

Task 22

The Rothertown bypass

New bypass will **harm wildlife!**

A major new bypass is planned to take traffic away from the centre of Rothertown in Sommershire. The new road will pass through a section of Ashworth Nature Reserve. The reserve is a Site of Special Scientific Interest (SSSI). It includes two ponds and a river. The reserve is home for lots of different animals, including roe deer and badgers.

The nature reserve

Your help is needed (by the local wildlife action group and the County Planning Department). They need to know:

- how the bypass will affect the environment.
- what can be done to protect the wildlife.

- Look at the photos on page 22.
- In your group, each choose an animal found in the reserve.
- Use books, CD-ROMs, the Internet and videos to find out as much as you can about your animal. For example:
  - What sort of habitat does it live in?
  - How does the habitat provide things that it needs?
  - Think about the food chain that helps it to stay alive.
- Each person in the group should prepare an information pack about the animal.
- In your group, discuss the advantages and disadvantages of the bypass for humans.

  You will need to use all of this information for the Checkpoint.
- Draw and write to show how wildlife might be affected. Use information from the whole group.

These are some of the animals that live in the Ashworth Nature Reserve

Stonefly

Mayfly

Frog

Badger

Newt

Freshwater shrimp

Shrew

Brown trout

Mole

Tawny owl

Field vole

Roe deer

Otter

Toad

Fox

Lesser spotted woodpecker

Rabbit

Checkpoint

Action plan

10

- In your group, look at the information you have collected for Task 22.
- Use this information to write an action plan on Task Sheet 10 for either:
  - the local wildlife group in Rothertown.
  - the warden of the nature reserve.
  - the road planners.
- In your plan, include:
  - a map to show where this action could take place.
  - how animals would be affected by the new bypass – you may need to use the words **habitat** and **food chain** in your report.
  - the advantages and disadvantages of the bypass for humans.
- When you have finished, compare your group's action plan with other groups in your class.

Rothertown bypass Action plan	
Map to show where action should be taken:	
Animals affected:	
Foxes will try to cross the road to get to the farm.	
Effect on the people of Rothertown:	
Advantages	*Disadvantages*
Less traffic in the town centre.	Road cuts through the footpath.
Suggestions for action to be taken:	

Summary

Which of these do you know and which can you do?

- I know that plants and animals are different living things.
- I know that different animals are found in different habitats.
- I can predict what organisms might be found in a habitat.
- I can observe a local habitat and record the animals found.
- I know that living things are adapted to their habitats.
- I can group organisms by how they look.
- I can use a key to identify plants and animals.
- I can identify a food chain.
- I know that most food chains start with a green plant.

Complete the **Science Log** to show how well you know these and how well you can do them. Circle a face for each statement.